ABOUT THE PUBLISHER

MICROCOSM PUBLISHING is Portland's most diversified publishing house and distributor, with a focus on the colorful, authentic, and empowering. Our books and zines have put your power in your hands since 1996, equipping readers to make positive changes in their lives and in the world around them. Microcosm emphasizes skill-building, showing hidden histories, and fostering creativity through challenging conventional publishing wisdom with books and bookettes about DIY skills, food, bicycling, gender, self-care, and social justice. What was once a distro and record label started by Joe Biel in a drafty bedroom was determined to be *Publishers Weekly*'s fastest-growing publisher of 2022 and #3 in 2023, and is now among the oldest independent publishing houses in Portland, OR, and Cleveland, OH. We are a politically moderate, centrist publisher in a world that has inched to the right for the past 80 years.

Global labor conditions are bad, and our roots in industrial Cleveland in the '70s and '80s made us appreciate the need to treat workers right. Therefore, our books are MADE IN THE USA.

"I have read the most fantastically inflated statistics of witch-hunt victims in all sorts of feminist journals, magazines and books. I once made the mistake myself of referring to 'hundreds of thousands' of women in an article about witchcraft. I now realise such figures are quite misleading. Even worse is the attribution of nine million victims which is flung about in feminist discussions of witchcraft with wild abandon, although *where it comes from, nobody knows.*"

— Lynette Mitchell, *Trouble & Strife*,
No. 2 (Spring 1984), pp. 19-20

Trouble & Strife was a radical feminist magazine published in Leeds, England. Mitchell's essay "Enemies of God or Victims of Patriarchy?" is available online: https://www.troubleandstrife. org/articles/issue-02

I made this zine to try to answer Mitchell's implied question: how did we end up thinking that nine million women were executed as witches?

Links to primary sources are in the endnotes. Reliable sources are cited in-text, and links to them are in Works Cited. Check them out!

— R.J. Gillis
June 27, 2023

Girls just want to have fun.
Hans Baldung Grien, *The Witches* (1510)
https://www.metmuseum.org/art/collection/search/416796

W.I.T.C.H. (Women's International Terrorist Conspiracy from Hell) may have been considered a "fringe" group within the women's movement when it debuted on Halloween 1968, but the archetype of the witch was increasingly taken up by feminists throughout the 1970s (Adler 1979/2006: 181-2). The group's manifesto, which had circulated in mimeograph form, was published in W.I.T.C.H. co-founder Robin Morgan's 1970 anthology *Sisterhood Is Powerful*:

> Witches have always been women who dared to be: groovy, courageous, aggressive, intelligent, nonconformist, explorative, curious, independent, sexually liberated, revolutionary. (This possibly explains why nine million of them have been burned.)[1]

Barbara Ehrenreich and Deirdre English's influential early-70s pamphlet *Witches, Midwives, and Nurses* credited "many writers" with estimating the number of accused witches killed during the early modern period (1500–1800) to have been "in the millions."[2] The claim that nine million people—the vast majority of them women—were killed in witch-hunts during the sixteenth and seventeenth centuries appeared again in *Ms.* magazine in 1974.[3] Given that modern scholars peg witch-hunt deaths at 40,000 (Scarre and Callow 2001: 21),[4] where did this gross exaggeration come from?

The *Ms.* article was an edited excerpt of "Gynocide: The Witches" from Andrea Dworkin's *Woman Hating*, which was published that same year.[5] Although Dworkin does not provide a citation for the "nine million" figure in either *Ms.* or *Woman Hating*, she does include *Witchcraft* by Pennethorne Hughes in the *Ms.* article's reference list. That work, first published in 1952,[6] asserts,

"The number who died as witches is purely problematical [sic]. Someone has suggested nine millions. It may be more."[7] But who was "someone"?

The "nine million witch-hunt victims" factoid was created by eighteenth-century German historian Gottfried Christian Voigt in a 1783 essay warning against the dangers of superstition (Behringer 1998). Voigt examined the archives in his town of Quedlinburg and found records for 30 witch trial executions during the 30-year period 1569-98. Voigt assumed that (1) the archives were incomplete and therefore he should increase the number of executions by one-third, and (2) those years were representative of the intensity of witch-hunting in Quedlinburg throughout its entire history, yielding 133 witches executed in Quedlinburg each century, for a total of 866 since its founding. He continued to extrapolate from there, assuming that a similar number of witches, proportional to population, were executed across Europe at a constant rate over eleven centuries. The result: nine million four hundred and forty-two thousand nine hundred and ninety-four victims. This was rounded down to a tidy nine million by Austrian theologian Georg Gustav Roskoff in his 1869 work *History of the Devil* (Behringer 1998: 670; Hutton 2003: 30; Bailey 2007: 238).

The nine-million figure may have first entered American feminist consciousness in 1893, when suffragist Matilda Joslyn Gage included it in *Woman, Church, and State: A Historical Account of the Status of Woman through the Christian Ages*.[8] Gage's themes are central to Ehrenreich and English's *Witches, Midwives, and Nurses* (Hasted 1984: 12; Hasted 1985: 22). Mary Daly quotes Gage's "nine million" directly in 1978's *Gyn/Ecology: The Metaethics of Radical Feminism*.[9] Daly is so taken with prospect of an early modern "gynocide" that she sees it as both preceding and in some ways superseding the Holocaust:

> [T]hose who write and speak of the holocaust of the Jews in twentieth-century Nazi Germany never acknowledge the history of gynocidal holocaust...The witch trials in Germany were characterized by extreme brutality combined with masterful meticulousness. Yet most authors...write about the massacre of the Jews as if such massive sadism were without this historical precedent.[10]

This brings us to the uses that Voigt's factoid was put to in Germany. In the 1830s and '40s, in response to Enlightenment-types like Voigt using the witch trials to attack the church, scholars with clerical sympathies suggested that "some elements of traditional witchcraft were based on pre-Christian Germanic traditions" and therefore ecclesiastical authorities had been right to suppress them (Bailey 2007: 240-1; see also Hutton 2014: 192-3). Later in the nineteenth century, the "nine million" figure was again used to attack the church as superstitious, this time by allies of German chancellor Otto von Bismarck in his *Kulturkampf* ("culture struggle") against the Roman Catholic Church (Behringer 1998: 671; Hutton 2003: 30).

During the 1920s, "nine million executed as witches" changed from a rationalist Protestant cudgel to a National Socialist one (Behringer 1998: 673-4). The theory that the witch trials had targeted followers of an underground pre-Christian religion received widespread attention following the 1921 publication of British Egyptologist Margaret Murray's *The Witch-Cult in Western Europe*.[11] The witch cult hypothesis fueled pagan-inclined Nazis' imaginings of an authentic Germanic religion independent from Christianity, which had, after all, emerged from Judaism. *Völkisch-*

movement[12] leader Mathilde Ludendorff amplified the claim that the witch-hunts had nine million—now specifically Aryan female—victims in a 1934 pamphlet titled *Christian Cruelty to German Women* (Behringer 1998: 674; Bailey 2007: 237-8). Believers in this gynocide included Nazi leaders: in 1935, Heinrich Himmler founded an SS unit charged with researching the persecution of witches (Sebald 1989: 253-4; Behringer 1998: 675; Bailey 2007: 236; Badger and Purkiss 2017: 127-8).

Himmler's *Hexen-Sonderauftrag* ("witch special mission") unit searched archives for nine years, yet amassed only 30,000 one-page dossiers on accused witches (Behringer 1998: 675-6; Sebald 1989: 257). Some of the entries were duplicates, while others referenced fictional sources (Sebald 1989: 258, Badger and Purkiss 2017: 137). Despite their flaws, the files were "the most systematic survey of witch trials ever made over a large area" (Bailey 2007: 236). That area included most of the Holy Roman Empire (a.k.a., the First Reich), home to six out of every seven witches executed between 1560 and 1660 (Monter 2002: 16). The *Hexenkartothek* ("witch card library"), cross-checked against the archives that survived World War II, is an important source for modern estimates of witch-hunt victims (Monter 2002: 13-15; Bailey 2007: 236). Thus the search for nine million led to only 40,000.

No doubt those authors who continue to claim that millions of women were burned as witches would be mortified to learn that they are echoing Nazi propaganda. Gently teach the real story when you can.

The Burning Times, a 1990 Canadian documentary, in which the early modern witch-hunts are called a "women's holocaust" with millions of victims. https://www.youtube.com/watch?v=34ow_kNnoro&t=856s

Endnotes

[1] Page 539 in *Sisterhood Is Powerful*, which is available online: https://www.archive.org/details/sisterhoodispowe00morg

[2] Pp. 7-8 in the 1973 printing of *Witches, Midwives, and Nurses*, which is available online (https://www.archive.org/details/witchesmidwivesn00ehre). The Feminist Press reissued *Witches, Midwives, and Nurses* as a "contemporary classic" in 2010.

[3] Page 52 in Dworkin, Andrea. 1974. "What Were Those Witches Really Brewing?" *Ms.* 2(10): 52-55, 89-90 (https://www.archive.org/details/ms02jamsfon5pa/page/n379): "Although statistical information on the witchcraft persecutions is very incomplete, the most reasonable estimate of the number executed on the whole of the Continent and the British Isles from 1484 until the end of the 17th century would seem to be 9 million. It may well have been more. The ratio of women to men executed has been variously estimated at 20 to 1 and 100 to 1. Witchcraft was a woman's crime."

[4] "It seems reasonable to accept the maximum figure of 40,000 executions, conducted across Europe from 1428 to 1782, which has been consistently advanced – and agreed upon – by such leading authorities as Berhringer, Briggs, Hutton, and Sharpe" (Scarre and Callow 2001: 21). Levack (1987: 21), who estimated 60,000 in the first edition of *The Witch-Hunt in Early Modern Europe* – a figure that is often used as the high end of "reasonable" estimates; for example, *Encyclopedia Britannica*'s limit of "no more than 40,000 to 60,000" (Russell and Lewis 2000) – revised his estimate down to 45,000 in the book's third edition (2006: 23). See also Hutton 1991: 306, 370; Golden 1997: 234; Hutton 1999: 132, 435-6; Monter 2002: 12-16. The number of trials was approximately double the number of executions (Levack 2006: 22-3; Monter 2002: 13).

[5] *Woman Hating* is available online: https://www.archive.org/details/womanhating00dwor/page/118

[6] *Witchcraft's* 1952 publication predates the 1954 publication of *Witchcraft Today* by Wicca founder Gerald Gardner, which asserts, "[I]t is estimated that nine million people were tortured to death during the persecution in Europe" (p. 38, 1970 printing: https://www.archive.org/details/witchcrafttoday0000gard/page/38). Since Gardner includes *Witchcraft* in his bibliography, that may be his source for the figure.

[7] Page 195 in the 1970 printing of *Witchcraft*, available online: https://www.archive.org/details/witchcraft00hugh/page/195

[8] Page 247 in *Woman, Church, and State*, which is available online (https://www.archive.org/details/womanchurchstate00gagerich/page/247): "It is computed from historical records that nine millions of persons were put to death for witchcraft after 1484, or during a period of three hundred years, and this estimate does not include the vast number who were sacrificed in the preceding centuries upon the same accusation."
    In *The Triumph of the Moon*, published in 1999 and therefore researched without the benefit of the vast digitized archives we now enjoy, Ronald Hutton, following Rachel Hasted's work in *Trouble & Strife*, credited Gage with inventing the figure (p. 141). He corrected this in 2003's *Witches, Druids, and King Arthur* (p. 30) after being made aware of Behringer 1998.

[9] Page 183 in *Gyn/Ecology*, which is available online: https://www.archive.org/details/gynecologymetaet0000daly/page/183

[10] Ibid, pp. 200-1.

[11] *The Witch-Cult in Western Europe* is available online: https://www.archive.org/details/x-witch-cult-in-western-europe

[12] "Folkist" movement, a German ethno-nationalist movement.

Witch feeding her familiars (1579)
https://publicdomainreview.org/essay/woodcuts-and-witches

Works Cited

Adler, Margot. 1979/2006. *Drawing Down the Moon: Witches, Druids, Goddess-Worshippers and Other Pagans in America.* New York: Penguin (https://www.archive.org/details/drawingdownmoonw0000adle).

Badger, William and Diane Purkiss. 2017. "English Witches and SS Academics: Evaluating Sources for the English Witch Trials in Himmler's Hexenkartothek." *Preternature* 6(1): 125-153. doi: 10.5325/preternature.6.1.0125 (https://research.uca.ac.uk/3283/8/HexenArtikel.pdf).

Bailey, Michael D. 2007. *Magic and Superstition in Europe: A Concise History from Antiquity to the Present.* Lanham, MD: Rowman & Littlefield.

Behringer, Wolfgang. 1998. "Neun Millionen Hexen: Entstehung, Tradition und Kritik eines populären Mythos." *Geschichte in Wissenschaft und Unterricht* 49: 664-685 (https://www.ludwig-neidhart.de/Downloads/HexenBehringer.pdf).

Golden, Richard M. 1997. "Satan in Europe: The Geography of Witch-Hunts." Pp. 216-47 in *Changing Identities in Early Modern France*, edited by Michael Wolfe. Durham, NC: Duke University Press.

Hasted, Rachel. 1984. "The New Myth of the Witch." *Trouble & Strife* 2: 10-17 (https://www.troubleandstrife.org/articles/issue-02).

Hasted, Rachel. 1985. "Mothers of Invention." *Trouble & Strife* 7: 17-25 (https://www.troubleandstrife.org/articles/issue-07).

Hutton, Ronald. 1991. *The Pagan Religions of the Ancient British Isles.* Oxford: Blackwell.

Hutton, Ronald. 1999. *The Triumph of the Moon: A History of Modern Pagan Witchcraft.* Oxford: Oxford University Press (https://www.archive.org/details/triumphofmoonhis0000hutt).

Hutton, Ronald. 2003. *Witches, Druids, and King Arthur.* London: Hambledon and London (https://www.archive.org/details/witchesdruidskin00hutt).

Hutton, Ronald. 2014. "Witchcraft and Modernity." Pp. 191-211 in *Writing Witch-Hunt Histories: Challenging the Paradigm,* edited by Marko Nenonen and Raisa Maria Toivo. Leiden, NL: Brill.

Levack, Brian P. 1987. *The Witch-Hunt in Early Modern Europe.* London: Longman (https://www.archive.org/details/witchhuntinearly0000leva).

Levack, Brian P. 2006. *The Witch-Hunt in Early Modern Europe.* 3rd ed. Harlow, UK: Pearson (https://www.archive.org/details/witchhuntinearly0000leva_l1l1).

Monter, William. 2002. "Witch Trials in Continental Europe, 1560-1660." Pp. 1-52 in *Witchcraft and Magic in Europe.* Vol. 4, *The Period of the Witch Trials,* edited by Bengst Ankarloo and Stuart Clark. Philadelphia: University of Pennsylvania Press.

Russell, Jeffrey Burton, and Ioan M. Lewis. 2000. "Witchcraft." *Encyclopedia Britannica.* Retrieved Aug. 27, 2021 (https://www.britannica.com/topic/witchcraft).

Scarre, Geoffrey and John Callow. 2001. *Witchcraft and Magic in Sixteenth- and Seventeenth-Century Europe*. 2nd ed. New York: Palgrave Macmillan.

Sebald, Hans. 1989. "Nazi Ideology Redefining Deviants: Witches, Himmler's Witch-trial Survey, and the Case of the Bishopric of Bamberg." *Deviant Behavior* 10(3): 253-270 (https://doi.org/10.1080/01639625.1989.9967814).

Woodcut from *The History of Witches and Wizards* (1720)
https://publicdomainreview.org/essay/woodcuts-and-witches

Typeset in Crimson Pro and Crimson Text on Affinity Publisher 2. Title font is Women's Car Repair Collective, which is inspired by hand-lettered feminist flyers of the 1970s (https://eyeondesign.aiga.org/womens-car-repair-collective).

SUBSCRIBE!

For as little as $15/month, you

can support a small, independent

publisher and get every book that we

publish—delivered to your doorstep!

www.**Microcosm.Pub/BFF**